The Homeschool
High School
Science

Notebooking Journal

This Book Belongs To:

A Sixteen Unit Journal for the Young Scientist

Anna Travis

The Homeschool High School Science Journal
Rethink Schooling, Vol. 9
A Sixteen Module Journal for the Young Scientist

© 2019 Anna Travis

ISBN: 9781708983550

Sweet Messy Faith Publishing
www.sweetmessyfaith.com
www.annatravis.com

If you enjoy this Journal,

please leave a review on amazon.com.

Thank you!

How to Use This Journal:

This journal is an attempt at simplicity. We designed it for our family to use with our favorite science curriculums. My high schoolers enjoy journaling what they learn, and creating our own science journal gave us a balance of freedom and guidance.

Each module has spaces for scientists to record the theme of the week, new vocabulary, drawings, observations, and fascinating facts.

My teens love to start with a broad topic and then follow their different interests. For example, your scientist can study the ocean. Then move on to specifics, such as whales, fish, weather, pollution, or shells. If your student is fascinated by whales, let them linger over the subject for as many weeks as they can continue to journal about, and then move on. If your curriculum leads you into an area that is not as fascinating, you can do a module (or not!) and then move on!

This approach works with a core curriculum or a raid-the-library approach. Have fun with it, and don't forget to jot down each module's theme in the Table of Contents. Enjoy!

Table of Contents:

Module:	Subject:
1	
2	
3	
4	
5	
6	
7	
8	
9	
10	
11	
12	
13	
14	
15	
16	

MODULE 1

Vocabulary

MODULE 1

Vocabulary

MODULE 1

Vocabulary

MODULE 1

Vocabulary

MODULE 1

Fascinating Facts

_____
_____
_____
_____
_____
_____
_____
_____
_____
_____
_____
_____

_____
_____
_____
_____
_____
_____
_____
_____
_____
_____
_____
_____

Fascinating Facts

MODULE 1

Notes:

Fascinating Facts

MODULE 1

Fascinating Facts

MODULE 1

Notes:

Draw & Label

MODULE 2

Vocabulary

MODULE 2

Vocabulary

MODULE 2

Vocabulary

MODULE 2

Vocabulary

MODULE 2

Fascinating Facts

_____
_____
_____
_____
_____
_____
_____
_____
_____
_____
_____
_____
_____

_____
_____
_____
_____
_____
_____
_____
_____
_____
_____
_____
_____
_____
_____

Fascinating Facts

MODULE 2

Notes:

Draw & Label

Fascinating Facts

MODULE 2

Fascinating Facts

MODULE 2

Notes:

Draw & Label

MODULE 3

Vocabulary

MODULE 3

Vocabulary

MODULE 3

Vocabulary

MODULE 3

Vocabulary

MODULE 3

Fascinating Facts

MODULE 3

Fascinating Facts

MODULE 3

Notes:

Draw & Label

Fascinating Facts

MODULE 3

Fascinating Facts

MODULE 3

Notes:

MODULE 4

Vocabulary

MODULE 4

Vocabulary

MODULE 4

Vocabulary

MODULE 4

Vocabulary

MODULE 4

Fascinating Facts

Fascinating Facts

MODULE 4

Notes:

Draw & Label

Fascinating Facts

MODULE 4

Fascinating Facts

_____
_____
_____
_____
_____
_____
_____
_____
_____
_____
_____
_____

_____
_____
_____
_____
_____
_____
_____
_____
_____
_____
_____
_____

MODULE 4

Notes:

Draw & Label

MODULE 5

Vocabulary

MODULE 5

Vocabulary

MODULE 5

Vocabulary

MODULE 5

Vocabulary

MODULE 5

Fascinating Facts

Fascinating Facts

MODULE 5

Notes:

MODULE 5

Fascinating Facts

MODULE 5

Fascinating Facts

MODULE 5

Notes:

Draw & Label

MODULE 6

Vocabulary

MODULE 6

Vocabulary

MODULE 6

Vocabulary

MODULE 6

Vocabulary

MODULE 6

Fascinating Facts

Fascinating Facts

MODULE 6

Notes:

Draw & Label

Fascinating Facts

MODULE 6

Fascinating Facts

MODULE 6

Notes:

Draw & Label

MODULE 7

Vocabulary

MODULE 7

Vocabulary

MODULE 7

Vocabulary

MODULE 7

Vocabulary

MODULE 7

Fascinating Facts

Fascinating Facts

MODULE 7

Notes:

Draw & Label

Fascinating Facts

MODULE 7

Fascinating Facts

_____

_____

_____

_____

_____

_____

_____

_____

_____

_____

_____

_____

_____

_____

_____

_____

_____

_____

_____

_____

_____

_____

MODULE 7

Notes:

Draw & Label

MODULE 8

Vocabulary

MODULE 8

Vocabulary

MODULE 8

Vocabulary

MODULE 8

Vocabulary

MODULE 8

Fascinating Facts

MODULE 8

Fascinating Facts

MODULE 8

Notes:

Draw & Label

MODULE 8

Fascinating Facts

MODULE 8

Fascinating Facts

MODULE 8

Notes:

Draw & Label

MODULE 9

Vocabulary

MODULE 9

Vocabulary

MODULE 9

Vocabulary

MODULE 9

Vocabulary

Fascinating Facts

MODULE 9

Fascinating Facts

MODULE 9

Notes:

Draw & Label

MODULE 9

Fascinating Facts

Fascinating Facts

MODULE 9

Notes:

Draw & Label

MODULE 10

Vocabulary

MODULE 10

Vocabulary

MODULE 10

Vocabulary

MODULE 10

Vocabulary

Fascinating Facts

MODULE 10

Fascinating Facts

MODULE 10

Notes:

Draw & Label

MODULE 10

Fascinating Facts

_____

_____

_____

_____

_____

_____

_____

_____

_____

_____

_____

_____

_____

_____

_____

_____

_____

_____

_____

_____

_____

_____

_____

_____

_____

Fascinating Facts

MODULE 10

Notes:

Draw & Label

MODULE 11

Vocabulary

MODULE 11

Vocabulary

MODULE 11

Vocabulary

MODULE 11

Vocabulary

Fascinating Facts

MODULE 11

Fascinating Facts

MODULE 11

Notes:

Draw & Label

MODULE 11

Fascinating Facts

_____
_____
_____
_____
_____
_____
_____
_____
_____
_____
_____

_____
_____
_____
_____
_____
_____
_____
_____
_____
_____
_____
_____

Fascinating Facts

MODULE 11

Notes:

Draw & Label

MODULE 12

Vocabulary

MODULE 12

Vocabulary

MODULE 12

Vocabulary

MODULE 12

Vocabulary

Fascinating Facts

MODULE 12

Fascinating Facts

MODULE 12

Notes:

Draw & Label

MODULE 12

Fascinating Facts

Fascinating Facts

MODULE 12

Notes:

Draw & Label

MODULE 13

Vocabulary

MODULE 13

Vocabulary

MODULE 13

Vocabulary

MODULE 13

Vocabulary

Fascinating Facts

MODULE 13

Fascinating Facts

MODULE 13

Notes:

Draw & Label

MODULE 13

Fascinating Facts

_____

_____

_____

_____

_____

_____

_____

_____

_____

_____

_____

_____

_____

_____

_____

_____

_____

_____

_____

_____

_____

_____

_____

_____

Fascinating Facts

MODULE 13

Notes:

Draw & Label

MODULE 14

Vocabulary

MODULE 14

Vocabulary

MODULE 14

Vocabulary

MODULE 14

Vocabulary

Fascinating Facts

MODULE 14

Fascinating Facts

MODULE 14

Notes:

Draw & Label

MODULE 14

Fascinating Facts

_____

_____

_____

_____

_____

_____

_____

_____

_____

_____

_____

_____

_____

_____

_____

_____

_____

_____

_____

_____

_____

_____

_____

_____

Fascinating Facts

MODULE 14

Notes:

Draw & Label

MODULE 15

Vocabulary

MODULE 15

Vocabulary

MODULE 15

Vocabulary

MODULE 15

Vocabulary

Fascinating Facts

MODULE 15

Fascinating Facts

MODULE 15

Notes:

Draw & Label

MODULE 15

Fascinating Facts

Fascinating Facts

MODULE 15

Notes:

Draw & Label

MODULE 16

Vocabulary

MODULE 16

Vocabulary

MODULE 16

Vocabulary

MODULE 16

Vocabulary

Fascinating Facts

MODULE 16

Fascinating Facts

MODULE 16

Notes:

Draw & Label

MODULE 16

Fascinating Facts

Fascinating Facts

MODULE 16

Notes:

Draw & Label

Printed in Poland
by Amazon Fulfillment
Poland Sp. z o.o., Wrocław

25808467R10094